LIFE UNDER THE FREEWAY

(and other points in time)

By: Rick Fontes

YESTERDAYS ARE FOREVER

Moments shared
Scattered here
Scattered there

Moments stolen from now
Pieced and fitted together
Form a never to be forgotten then

Make the most of these moments

For today
Turns the promise of tomorrow
Into yesterdays

And yesterdays

Only yesterdays

Are forever

Reprinted from "ELEMENTS"
BY: Sharon Wright & Rick Fontes

Life Under the Freeway

Published by Lulu.Com

ISBN 978-0-557-47537-7

This book is a journey and I thank you for joining me as I attempt to trace the steps leading from that long ago, to this present place.

Along the path there were many to thank, and a few to bless and forget.

I have had good family and good friends, without whose support this life might not have endured.

I especially thank my wife, Ruth. She is the one who stayed and helped to point a direction at the time when a direction was truly needed.

And to my mom, Vivian, thanks for planting the seeds and keeping the faith.

I do not claim that the following pages contain great literature.

They are merely glimpses into the soul of a single individual as he slouches toward some form of awareness

I hope that you find something of interest along the path.

TABLE OF CONTENTS:

PROLOGUE

I once wrote a book.
Family and friends
All bought duty copies.

My ego soared to new heights.

And yet the the world went into depression.
Corruption in government rose.
Across the planet children still faced starvation.
Pollution reached new levels.

Perhaps if I were to write another book.

TO MEL:
AN EXCUSE FOR THE IMMATURITY
YOU
HATE SO.

Sorry.

It isn't possible for me
To love you exclusively.

How could I exclude
Springtime?
Roses?
New wine?

KITTENS AND PLANTS

Each lovable in its own way
Each asking just a little of your time
Time that I jealously hoard for myself.

How can a rational man
Envy a few strokes
Given a droopy leafed fern
&
A scruffy black and white mouser?

REDUNDANCY

Why this need
To have "ourness" defined?

Has not the sharing
Spoken eloquently
Of the real unreality of it all?

INTRODUCTION

Some would call it "reflection."
This trailing through my mind,
Looking for traces of you.

I find a hurried touch,
Your sigh,
A casual glance.

A meeting of our eyes
Canceling the crowd.

Are we in love?
Were we in Love?
Or does it even matter?

Would defining it
Somehow change it?

A part of me is gone
But the only thing missing
Is you.

LOVE STORY

If I ripped out my guts
And left them in a box
In the corner of your room

Would you at least Look at them
Now and again?

ANYTHING

Sometimes it's just over.

One moment it's there.
Surrounding you.
Totally you.

It has always been.
It is.
It will always be.

Then it's over.

Sad.

PRESSURE COOKER

Lunch with Tom Collins and a twist.
Slotted coins buying push button romance.
Flashing back-bar neon.

Giggling, staggering out into the noon light.

Double-eagled, chrome plated,
Velour upholstered, conjugal couch.

Bar rooms to back seats.

A well traveled route
That took you away
From our two-car, split-level
Suburban dream.

DAWN'S EARLY LITANY

Fishing for any excuse
To explain
Why I'm eight hours late.

I'd say "overtime'
But you'd call the plant.

I'd say "car trouble"
Or "flat tire"
But you'd check it out.

I could say
"Forty pounds overweight
And five kids"

But the truth is hurtful.

So you go on and bitch.

I'll just play "passed out."

FOR TERRI

Furious flight
Through nighttime places
Seeking,
Searching.

Doors swinging in.
Doors swinging out.

Not here again.
Not there again.

I promised.
Oh God how I promised,

To never again prowl
Through this neon-splashed demi-world,
Begging you to come home.

(more)

FOR TERRI (cont.)

I must need this rejection
Just as you need your freedom

In the warm glow,
Of sun-bright day,
I function with ease.

Rationality reigns.

I do not need you
I do not need your love-lies.

You are near
And yet I ignore your presence.

The sun sets.
Anxiety rises.
You exit.
Pride dies.

Again I become
A seeker in the night.

HELPMEET

My granddaddy castrated goats
The old country way.

He would bite off their balls
And swallow them.

You could've taught him
The power of the spoken word.

LONG ISLAND BLUES

Dog walking and toe stubbing my way
Through this loathsome suburban jungle
That your mini-skirted, tight-assed body
Sentenced me to,

Wishing to hell I was back in the past,
Still drinking and jiving at Sammy's Place,
And looking in some other direction
When you walked in.

I hate this dog.
Hate your crabgrass, too.

And it's been so long since you gave up,
The only thing there is to like about you,

I probably won't even like it anymore

NIGHT SEARCH

Searching night canyons.
Longing for any warmth
To fill this emptiness.

Imagination places the mask of your face
Onto whoever, whatever,
Emerges from the darkness

To ease the pain
Born of the price
That I pay for your freedom.

PRAYER TIME AT THE RODEWAY INN

Alone again.
Sick at heart again.

God, grant me more than this.
More than damp tangled sheets.
More than mindless
Mid-afternoon couplings
In airless roadside cubicles.

Send me a love of my own
To replace that which I steal
From within the circle
Of another man's ring.

FUTURE MEMORY

I know you well.
I know well
Those shimmering waves
Of chestnut brown
Which fall forward to cover an angel's smile.

I know you well.
I know well
The delicate, sensuous curve
Of your sculptured form.

I know you well.
I know well
The thrill of holding you close
Through a long, stormy night.

I know you well.
I know well
Your soft touch,
Your gentle caress.

Indeed, I know you well
But only in my dreams.

GEORGIA GIRL

I run screaming through the wind.
Flesh torn
By fingers of uncaring circumstance.

Refuge was found
In the cradle of your psyche,
Not really refuge, merely respite.

A seed torn too soon
From the sweet red earth.

Left to die unfulfilled.

INDIANA MOONLIGHT

Holding you.
Pretending to be not holding you.

Remembering those times
That simply passed on by.

I could easily say, "I love you"
And at this moment in time truly mean it.
And it would please you.

But this night's reality
Will never survive tomorrow's dawn.

TIME

Stretching toward eternity.

From out its dim recesses,
Calls two together, again and again.

The edge of memory,
Slicing keenly into nowness,
Has reclaimed you for me.

CIRCLES OUT OF SYNC

Circles,
Within circles,
Circling around and about.

Chasing, the chaser is chased.

Roles converging, reversing, merging.

Who needs?
Who wants?
Who ever.

Never is ever within reach.

Always on the opposite side of the circle,

Chasing.

AN OBSERVATION TO EXPLAIN WHY I AM SITTING HERE ALL ALONE ON A RAINY WEDNESDAY NIGHT WHILE YOU ARE OUT THERE SOMEWHERE IN THE VERY SAME TOWN IGNORING THE FACT THAT I AM ALIVE AND AM DESPERATELY NEEDING TO BE WITH YOU.

The opposite of love is not hate,
It's indifference.

PAINSURE

It hurts.

It hurts being on the edge of humanity,
Skimming lightly over a sea of feeling.

Able now to look only inward
Toward emptiness.

Silently screaming all the while,
In fear of exposed nerve endings,

Sensors once bathed in pleasure,
Now turned to pain,

By your final, self-serving stroke.

GROWTH (With apologies to Kris Kristofferson)

Turn loose my sleeve,
Bobby McGee.

The spectrum has shifted.

I no longer see
The delicate tones of your rainbow.

I have become blinded to your path,
And you to mine.

I'll think often of Salinas.

But there is a mountain
Yet unclimbed in New Mexico

And I've still to hear
The songs of Kankakee.

NEW MATH

You've taught me
 A new mathematical concept.

Two, divided by one,
Leaves a remainder of one.

A REMAINDER OF ONE

In my dream I call your name,
Lying here holding a wish for togetherness.

Unable to bridge the distance
Measured now in miles rather than inches.

Soon the moment of ecstasy.

Dream fuses to reality
Tensions release.

I begin to drift lazily,
A journey into that once shared twilight.

This is all that remains of us.

Solo dream
Solo love

Calling out your name.

HIGH ASPIRATIONS

Ever want to be a pirate?

Roam the seas?
Pillage and plunder?
Chests of gold?

Hook for a hand?
Patch over one eye?
A wooden peg leg?

Yet another opportunity
For the handicapped.

TO MY FATHER

How is it that I,
Having never known you,
Have become you?

CHRYSALIS (or whatever the hell that word is for when a butterfly leaves its cocoon)

Yesterday I stored away
My tattered, brown knit cap,
Useless now in this 72 degree weather.

So sad.

So like everything else in life.

From essential to unnecessary
In the space of just 40 degrees
On the Fahrenheit scale.

AN OBSERVATION IN PASSING

There is no real Springtime
 In the deep South.

Not exactly an earthshaking revelation.

I mention it only to express my regret.

LARRY'S POEM

Living under the freeway
Going quietly mad.

I wish that I could blame it all
On you that I'm sitting here.

Or on the sweet Thunderbird,
But I brought it here.

Or on this hole in my shoe,
But I walked it here.

Or on the whole bloody world
That I'm hiding from here.

I guess I'll just blame it on myself,
And end it here.

I'M NOT ASLEEP

Lying here on this sweat-soaked cot
In this Godforsaken flop,
Somewhere between New Jersey
And Nevermore.

And I'm not asleep.

Groping in trash filled corners
For those glassy friends
Long drained of their fear quenching potion.

And I'm not asleep.

Staring out through dirt-streaked windows
Seeing shackle-free clouds
Scudding across the full moon's face.

And I'm not asleep.

Knees tucked tight against chest,
Choking back a scream of terror.
Screaming: I'm not asleep.

(more)

I'M NOT ASLEEP (cont.)

Scaled bellies trail paths across the ceiling
While yellowed fanged rats
Wait patiently, hungrily for my sleep.

And I'm not asleep.

Sleep is buried now.
Dormant in a hillside plot since
Twenty lifetimes ago,
Its heart staked by a Judas kiss.

And sleep can come no more.

LIFE UNDER THE FREEWAY

It's Winter set.

Life under the freeway
Is bearable once more.

Robins play where yesterday
Only starving pigeons dared.

Gone is the cold on my skin,
Endured only by your sharing.

I welcome the moist sheen
Of too long stored poisons.

Perhaps now
I will be able to sweat out the poem
That has been building
Over the long grey Winter.

WHAT ARE YOU DOING HERE?

You've taken it all.

I've nothing left.

Happiness... gone,
Reputation... gone,
Health... gone,
Fame... gone,
Hope... gone.

I've nothing left but my sanity.

What?

Oh, I see.

Oh well,
What the hell,

How do you want it wrapped?

COMING DOWN

Strange.

I'm sure I left my mind

Somewhere in this room.

I thought I put it up on the closet shelf,

Before rolling that crisp dollar bill
And snorting my way to Xanadu.

Maybe I left it there, over in that far corner.

Or under the bed.

Or by the stove.

I just don't see it anywhere.

No problem, .

I never use it anyway.

AN EXCURSION INTO CENTRAL PARK

Hey you!!

Rich bitch!!

I'll bet that little silver poodle
Never eats from a garbage can.

WELL, I DO.

STREET DOG

A squeal of brakes.

Terminal thud.

Damp inquisitive nose nuzzling cold teats.

A taste of mother's milk commingled with
Blood.

Whimpering, tail tucked.

Slinking back into the safety of the alley.

Sudden weaning.

The first bitter lesson in the short,
Sad life of a street dog.

FROM THE MOSEL TO THE MOSELLE

River of wine flowing southward,
Through grape-laden hillsides,
To be absorbed
By unquenchable Gallic thirst.

The milk of your breast sustains,
Softens this curbstone into a pillow,
Opens the spillway of lost dreams

And wipes away
My South Chicago reality.

THE BARD OF THIRD AVENUE

There are more things
 In a bottle of muscatel
Than are dreamt of
 In all your philosophies,
Horatio.

STAR WORSHIP

I saw Loretta Lynn in person once.

Up in Cincinnati.

I bought a ticket and walked right in.

Hell, man, she's real people,
Just like you and me.

I'll betcha if she was here,
She'd front me a buck or two
On some Mad Dog 20-20.

TELL ME WHERE, SHEL

I read your book, man,
And I'm here to tell you,
Some sidewalks
Never end.

MORNING AFTER CONVERSION

Lord,
Now I ain't complaining
'Cause I know
Any damn fool crazy enough
To mix Gallo Port Wine and Everclear,
Deserves to feel like I do.

But, Lord,
Instead of making me work it all out,
All at the same time,

Couldn't you
Sort of back the pain off a couple notches
And spread it over a week or so?

PASSING THROUGH ATLANTA

I saw God
Walking down Peachtree Street.

He was wearing an old army jacket,
And had a sack of Bull Durham
In his hip pocket.

"The truth," I begged of him,
While tugging at his sleeve.

"Where can I find the meaning of life?"

"Hell," said he, "I don't know.
I'm just winging it like the rest of y'all."

FAMILY REUNION

I hiked across a nation,
To visit your hillside.

I lingered, awestruck, amid the stone forest,
Surrounded by the name
That I call myself.

A BLINK WHEN THE LIGHT COMES ON

The sign on the billboard says:

"Jesus Saves Sinners."

Just goes to show,
Some folks will collect anything.

NOWHERE TO HIDE

In Manhattan there are no trees to climb.

No place to hide from the Blue Meanies
That crawl the gutter places,

Eating the eyeballs of the hopeless.
The Down-slid.
These ex-temples of God.

THE BAG LADIES OF THE LOWER EAST SIDE

Little dumpy women people,
Abdicating grandmotherhood,
To roam the city's core.

Always searching.

A bit of string.
A half used matchbook.
The New York Times,
Now twenty-four hours into history.

Picking. Lifting. Scanning.

Turning each new treasure
In gnarled, age spotted hands

Judging. Rating. Deciding.

A keeper? Yes, definitely a keeper.

Stuff into the gaping maw
The insatiable mouth
Of the ever present shopping bag.

The dying picking among the dead.

NASHBOROUGH

Green in grey,
A tiny spot of rest
Which Cherokee ghosts watch
From across the mighty Cumberland
As vacuous tourists
Capture the fort
Their warrior arrows could never reach.

GYPSY WOMAN WRAPPED IN MINK

Lines in your hand
Scream denied potential
As you don gloves
Of unfurrowed skin
To hide the pain
Of knowing the Universal Truth

THE MAGICIAN OF HOGAN STREET

Giant red palm
Enameled and open to the world
Sees all, knows all, tells all

Bags of fragmented bones
Moldy, stinking chicken parts
A feather plucked
From some night flying bird

Strange bits
of foul smelling vegetation
Graveyard dust
Hoodoo, voodoo, mojo

And the ubiquitous, pale blue Cadillac

HOUSTON: A STUDY IN OLD HOUSES AND THUNDERSTORMS

Hidden from the rain,
Sleeping on the floor
Of an abandoned Montrose mansion

Safe, but far from satisfied.

Wishing I was back in Jersey City,
Tossing and cussing on a lumpy cot
In some downtown mission flop.

ON AGING

Sexy chicks stopped looking at me
Several summers and countless cities ago.

I still have the wine, the memories
and the occasional chance encounter
With someone from my salad days

From those times
before the magnetic road
Drew me away from home and hearth.

And the regrets.

I tried to go home, a time or two,
But he was always there,
Tom Wolfe, blocking the off-ramp.

A PRAYER FOR MORNING, EVENING AND IN BETWEEN

I want to scream,
"Oh God, help me, save me."

And to believe someone,
Somewhere,
Is listening
And might even care.

PERSPECTIVE

Life is everywhere
Even in the green slime
That covers the walls in this cell.

High above the stacked stone
A light filters in.

I climb toward that light,
Fingers torn, bleeding.

Slipping back.

Inching up once more.

Until at last, at long , long last,

I peer out through my own eyes.

MILESTONES

Beware the unknown terror,
That stalks our midnight,
Seeking to catch us unaware

Seeking to steal life

To leave us drained, as by a spider

A dry husk crying out “Danger!!!”
For the next blind passerby

THE SPECTRUM OF CONSCIOUSNESS

The Colors:

Red and Gold, Metallic blue, Magenta.

Cold Fire:

Lifting Us, Turning Us, Pulling Us.

Always Upward, Heaven Bound.

Terrified:

Clinging To The Wheel Of Life.

Screaming:

What? Why? Where?

You cannot know,

Nevertheless, you must go.

PERSPECTIVE OF A SIMPLER SORT

A single Indian paintbrush,
Growing on a remote hillside,
In some forgotten place
Between Austin and Lampasas,
Has more value
Than all the flower arrangements
In all the cathedrals of the world.

ERATO

I spent my Springtime looking for you.

Throughout the Summer of my life
I dreamed a dream of you

Each dawn began the quest anew.
Each sunrise renewed the hope
That you would appear.

Each pale-lit moon
Would close another empty page.

You were not to be found
Amid the pyramids of the Nile,
Nor camped among the Sherpas
In wind-swept Nepal.

(more)

ERATO (cont.)

Against the advice
Of those who thought you but a ghost,

I sailed to the valleys of Venus,
Strode the dry canals of Mars.

Time and space and hope and dreams
Became all one fabric.

Into the Fall of this life, heedless,
Unrequited I sped,

Calling out the name
That I hoped someday to give to you.

And now that Winter holds my heart
In an icy grip,

With daisy-garlanded head
You at last appear,

Your lips singing a siren's song.

BEGINDING

I'm out of it now.
The wine, the women
Even the memories.

Gone, all gone.

Replaced by the solitude
Of a forest glade.

Ducks in the pond where I bathe,
Reminiscent of those made of rubber
In a dimly remembered, childhood tub.

Animals, real now, not stuffed,
Nibble offerings at my cabin door.

And, again at bedtime,
A loving voice from above,
Assures me that tomorrow all will be well.

Full circle of sorts.

EPILOGUE: survival of the poet

I can never kill myself
So long as there remains
This compulsion to continually rewrite the note

THE END
(of the beginning)

www.ingramcontent.com/pod-product-compliance
Ingram Content Group UK Ltd.
Pitfield, Milton Keynes, MK11 3LW, UK
UKHW040557210726
13854UKWH00007B/1281

9 780557 475377